The Atlas of
Famous Battles
of the American
Revolution™

The Battle of Lexington and Concord

Scott P. Waldman

The Rosen Publishing Group's
PowerKids Press™
New York

Published in 2003 by The Rosen Publishing Group, Inc.
29 East 21st Street, New York, NY 10010
Copyright © 2003 by The Rosen Publishing Group, Inc.

First Edition

Editor: Nancy MacDonell Smith

Book Design: Michael J. Caroleo

Photo Credits: Cover, pp. 12, 15 (map) by Maria Melendez; cover, title page, p. 7 (General Gage) © Yale Center for British Art, Paul Mellon Collection, USA/Bridgeman Art Library; cover, title page, p. 8 (Paul Revere) courtesy, Museum of Fine Arts, Boston, reproduced with permission, © 2000 Museum of Fine Arts, Boston, All Rights Reserved; p. 4 (King George III) © Archivo Iconografico, S.A./CORBIS; pp. 4 (British trooper), 8 (minuteman farmer), 12 (minuteman, colonial troops), 14, 15 (inset), 16 (colonial troops) © North Wind Picture Archives; p. 4 (map) Map Division Library of Congress; pp. 4 (inset), 8 (Revere's ride) © Bettmann/CORBIS; pp. 7 (map), 8 (map), courtesy of Map Division, The New York Public Library, Astor, Lenox and Tilden Foundations; pp. 7 (carbine), 11 (musket) © George C. Neumann Collection, Valley Forge National Historic Park, photos by Cindy Reiman; p. 8 (Prescott) Emmett Collection, Miriam and Ira D. Wallach Division of Art, Prints and Photographs, The New York Public Library, Astor, Lenox and Tilden Foundations; pp. 11 (battle illustration), 12 (British troops and battle illustration), 15 (colonists illustration), 16 (British troops), 19 (battle illustration) Print Collection, Miriam and Ira D. Wallach Division of Art, Prints and Photographs, The New York Public Library, Astor, Lenox and Tilden Foundations; pp.11 (map), 16 (map), 19 (map), 20 (map) by Michael Jacobsen; p. 12 (top left) © Kevin Fleming/CORBIS; p. 16 (Percy) © SuperStock; p. 16 (cannon) © Lee Snider, Lee Snider/CORBIS; p. 19 (broadsheets) courtesy of American Antiquarian Society; p. 20 (insets) Phelps Stokes Collection, Miriam and Ira D. Wallach Division of Art, Prints and Photographs, The New York Public Library, Astor, Lenox and Tilden Foundations.

Waldman, Scott P.
The Battle of Lexington and Concord / by Scott P. Waldman.
    p. cm. — (The atlas of famous battles of the American
Revolution)
Includes bibliographical references and index.
Summary: A play-by-play description of the Battle of Lexington and Concord, using atlas-style maps and charts.
  ISBN 0–8239–6328–4 (lib. bdg.)
1. Lexington, Battle of, 1775—Juvenile literature. 2. Concord, Battle of, 1775—Juvenile literature. 3. Lexington, Battle of, 1775—Maps—Juvenile literature.
4. Concord, Battle of, 1775—Maps—Juvenile literature. [1. Lexington, Battle of, 1775—Maps. 2. Concord, Battle of, 1775—Maps. 3. United States—History—
Revolution, 1775–1783—Campaigns—Maps.] I. Title.
  E241.L6 W35 2003
  973.3'31—dc21

                                                                                           2001006030

Manufactured in the United States of America

Contents

1   Trouble Starts   5

2   The British Plan   6

3   Paul Revere's Ride   9

4   The Battle in Lexington   10

5   The Battle for North Bridge   13

6   A Different Kind of Battle   14

7   The Luck of the British Changes   17

8   The Burning of Menotomy   18

9   Counting the Dead   21

10   A Colony at War   22

Glossary   23

Index   24

Primary Sources   24

Web Sites   24

Trouble Starts

At the end of the eighteenth century, the 13 American colonies were ruled by George III, king of Great Britain. The **colonists** were not happy with his rule. The colonists disliked the British soldiers who were sent to make sure they obeyed the king's laws. The soldiers were known as **regulars**. On March 5, 1770, a group of colonists in Boston threw snowballs at some British soldiers. The soldiers shot five colonists. This became known as the Boston **Massacre**. Then the king raised the tax on tea. The angry colonists stole tea and dumped it into Boston Harbor. This became known as the Boston Tea Party. The colonists wanted to make their own laws. At a meeting called the **Continental Congress**, they decided that the only way to do this was to fight the British.

This map of the 13 colonies was made in 1774, one year before the Battle of Lexington and Concord. Inset: The Boston Tea Party (December 16, 1773) was one of the first acts of the American Revolution. Top: King George III tried to keep the colonists from rebelling. Bottom: The regulars' uniforms were red. The colonists, who didn't like the regulars, called them redcoats or lobsterbacks.

The British Plan

King George III sent Lieutenant General Thomas Gage, the commander in chief of the British army in North America, to Boston to become the **governor** of Massachusetts. Gage's job was to make sure the colonists obeyed the law. Spies warned Gage that the colonists were gathering **weapons** to fight the British. The king ordered Gage to take the weapons away from the colonists. Gage knew that, for this plan to succeed, it must be kept secret from the colonists. On the night of April 18, 1775, Gage gathered 700 soldiers and prepared to march into the town of Concord, Massachusetts. Gage did not want the colonists to gather weapons that they could use against his soldiers. He sent patrols into the countryside on the night of April 18 to stop messengers from spreading the word about his actions. The colonists were not so easily tricked, though. They were ready for the regulars.

The regulars marched from Boston to Concord, where the colonists had hidden weapons to fight the British. The regulars planned to capture these weapons.
Inset: At the start of the American Revolution, General Thomas Gage was the most powerful British official in the colonies.

Militia

Lexington

Lo_

Rock

Concord

Bridge where the
attack began

Col. Smiths return from Concord.

Monatomy

Militia

Provincials firing behind
the Walls

Bever Brook

P L A I N

Waltham

Water Town

Bridge

W A T E R   T O W N

OF THE
HARBOUR of
TON.
_nt with the Road
_ Concord
_e Engagement
_ the Provincials,
_cuampments of
_ston.
_Ac_ Survey

Weston

Water Town Hill

Head Quarters of the B___
encamped comman___

This gun, which was known as a carbine, is the kind that British soldiers carried during the American Revolution.

Paul Revere
is captured.

Samuel Prescott
begins his ride.

Samuel Prescott
warns Concord.

Paul Revere
begins his ride.

Paul Revere was a silversmith. In this portrait, he holds one of the teapots he made in his shop.

Paul Revere's Ride

Shortly before midnight on April 18, 1775, Paul Revere, a Boston silversmith, learned that Gage was planning to march from Boston to Concord. Revere arranged for two lanterns to be hung in a church, where they could be seen for miles (km) around. This was part of the colonists' plan to let neighboring towns know if the regulars marched inland from Boston. Two lit lanterns meant the regulars were coming by water. One meant they were coming by land. Revere then began an 18-mile (29-km) ride from Boston to Lexington and to Concord. He wanted to warn the citizens about the regulars. Revere was captured on his way to Concord. A local doctor, Samuel Prescott, was able to warn the town. The weapons were hidden. The colonists got ready for a battle. These colonists were members of the **militia**. Some militia members were known as **minutemen** because they could get ready very quickly.

This map shows the routes taken by Revere and Prescott. General Gage had soldiers on horseback along the road, but Prescott was able to get by them. Inset: The minutemen got their nickname from their ability to drop what they were doing and be ready for battle at a minute's notice.
Top: Samuel Prescott was the man who rode on to Concord after Paul Revere was captured.

The Battle in Lexington

At about 4:00 A.M. on April 19, 1775, Captain John Parker gathered 70 colonists to meet the regulars at Lexington Green. Parker was a local farmer with combat experience. Shortly before dawn, the British troops marched into view. Captain Parker ordered his men to **disperse** when he saw how outnumbered they were. As they were leaving, someone fired a **musket**. No one is sure from which side it came. Both sides began shooting at each other. By 5:00 A.M. the regulars had overpowered the colonists. Both minutemen and regulars were killed in the fighting. The regulars continued to march the 6 miles (10 km) to Concord. The battle left the colonists with an important decision to make. They could have returned to their homes and **submitted** to British rule. Instead they chose to fight for their rights. Captain Parker and his men left for Concord, where the battle would continue.

Top: *This map shows the routes taken by the colonists and the British as they fought in Lexington.*
Bottom: *This picture of the battle at Lexington Green was made by a Connecticut man named Amos Doolittle from eyewitness accounts two weeks after the battle.*

Above:
Today a re-creation of North Bridge stands exactly where the original was.

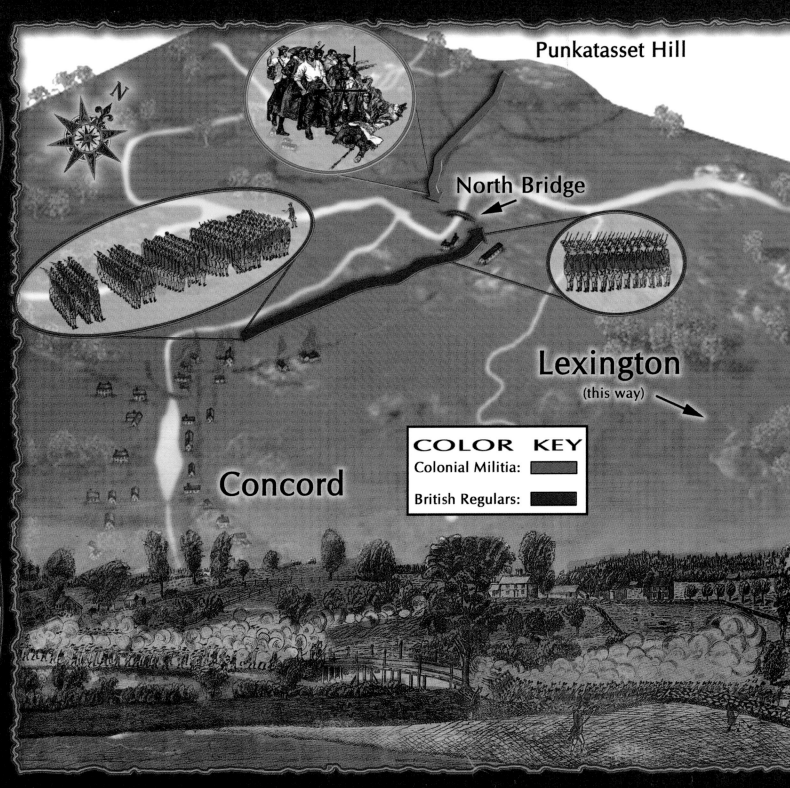

Punkatasset Hill

North Bridge

Lexington
(this way)

Concord

COLOR KEY

Colonial Militia:

British Regulars:

The Battle for North Bridge

The militia in Concord knew they were outnumbered by the British. At about 7:00 A.M., they decided not to defend the town. They retreated to a nearby hill overlooking the town. The British took control of Concord without firing a shot. They burned down the house where the colonists had hidden weapons. The fire from the house soon spread to the town hall. The militia saw the smoke and went back to defend the town. At about 9:30 A.M. the militia, who now numbered 450, reached North Bridge. This bridge was one of the main entrances into Concord. A group of about 96 regulars stood guard there. No one knows who began to shoot first. Two colonists and three British soldiers were killed. The militia took control of the North Bridge. Killing the regulars was a very daring thing to do. The colonists had **defied** the king. The first shot that killed a regular at North Bridge became known as the "shot heard 'round the world," because it changed history.

Top: This map shows how the colonists and the British moved in and around Concord.
Bottom: The fighting at North Bridge was a turning point in the battle because the colonists killed British soldiers for the first time. Far left, bottom: Once the militia heard that the British were marching to Concord, they hurried to defend the town.

A Different Kind of Battle

The militia kept arriving in Concord. The regulars decided to **retreat** when they realized 2,000 colonists had gathered in the town. At about noon, the regulars retreated back down the 18-mile (29-km) route from which they had come. About 1 mile (1.5 km) east of Concord, the colonists attacked the regulars. In the eighteenth century, armies would line up on either side of a battlefield to shoot at each other. The colonists did not do this. Instead they used fighting **techniques** that they had learned from Native Americans. They hid behind barns, trees, and rocks and fired at the British from all directions. They even ran ahead to shoot at the regulars as they approached. The colonists were not following the rules of battle. This angered and frightened the British. The British retreat turned into a run.

The colonists attacked the British from behind rocks, trees, and buildings. This was not done by most European armies at that time. Later on, however, this became a common way of fighting.

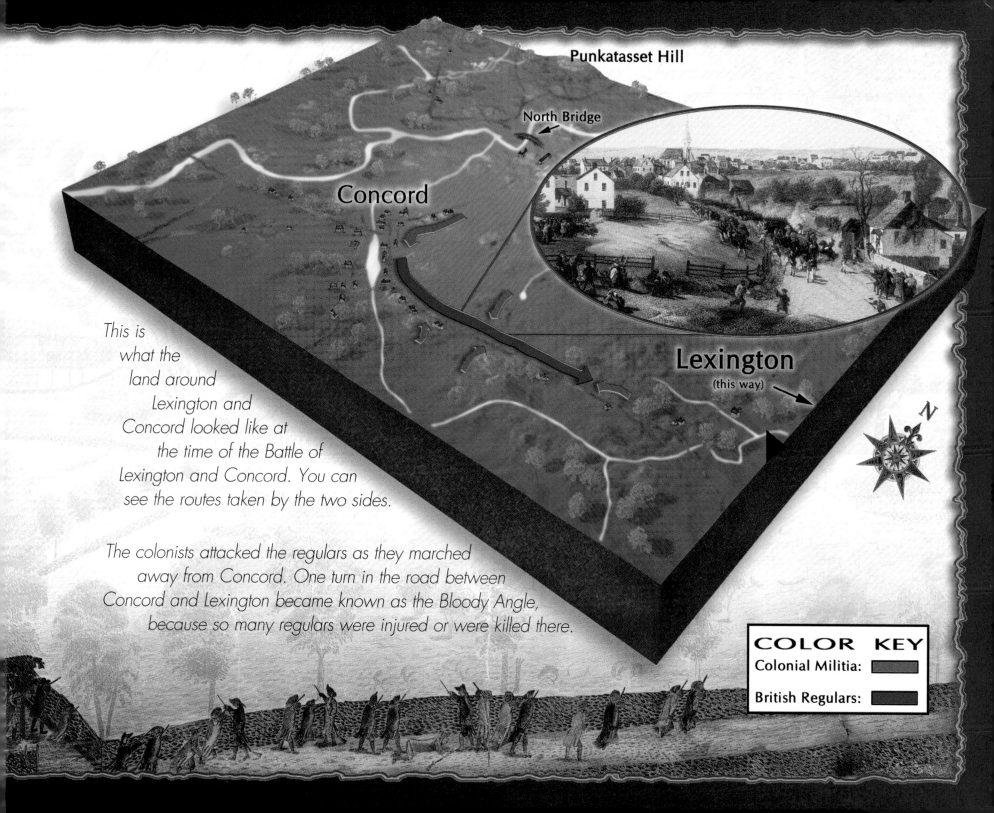

Punkatasset Hill

North Bridge

Concord

Lexington
(this way)

*This is
what the
land around
Lexington and
Concord looked like at
the time of the Battle of
Lexington and Concord. You can
see the routes taken by the two sides.*

*The colonists attacked the regulars as they marched
away from Concord. One turn in the road between
Concord and Lexington became known as the Bloody Angle,
because so many regulars were injured or were killed there.*

N

COLOR KEY

Colonial Militia:

British Regulars:

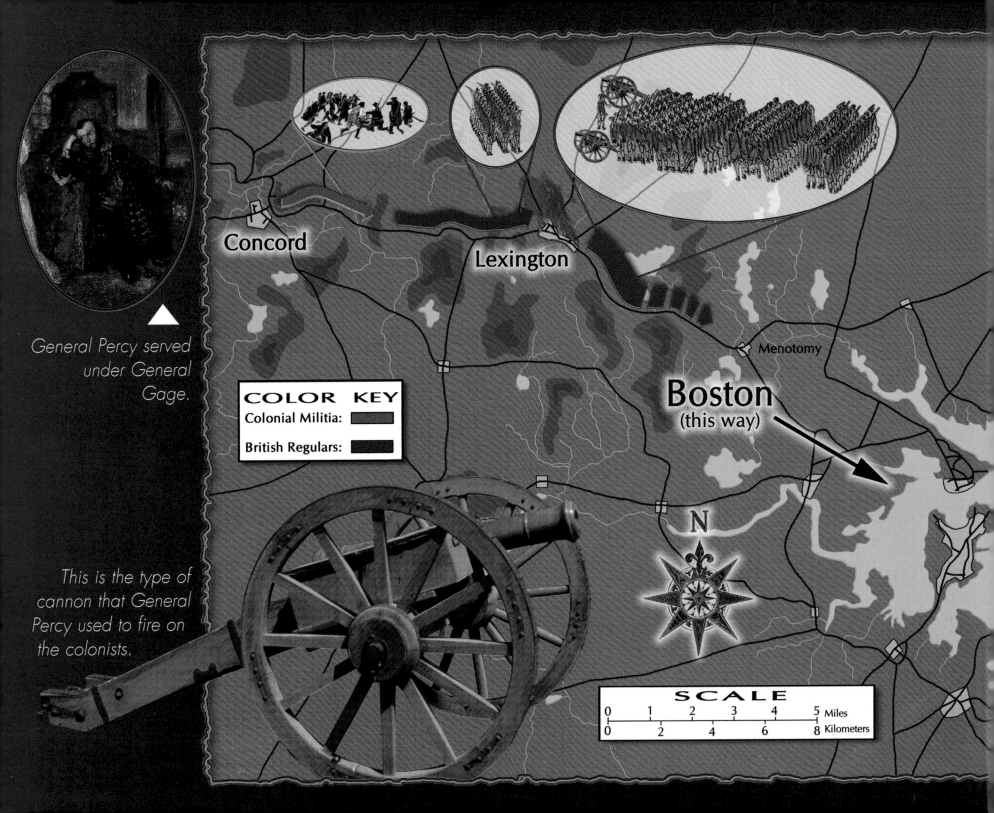

General Percy served under General Gage.

This is the type of cannon that General Percy used to fire on the colonists.

Concord

Lexington

Menotomy

Boston
(this way)

COLOR KEY

Colonial Militia:

British Regulars:

N

SCALE

| 0 | 1 | 2 | 3 | 4 | 5 | Miles |

| 0 | | 2 | | 4 | | 6 | | 8 | Kilometers |

The Luck of the British Changes

The regulars let out a cheer of **relief** when they reached Lexington at about 2:30 P.M. General Lord Hugh Percy, a British officer who had fought in many battles, was waiting for them. He had 1,000 British troops in battle **formation**, ready to fight. The general also had two cannons that he fired at the colonists, who were chasing the redcoats. The cannon fire confused the colonists, who were not used to battle. They scattered to keep from being shot. This briefly stopped their advance on the regulars. The British used the break to get even for the **sniper** fire they had suffered since leaving Concord. The regulars burned houses and stole from people in Lexington. After the attack on Lexington, General Percy got his troops together for the 12-mile (19-km) march to Boston. British navy ships were waiting for them in Boston Harbor. Meanwhile the colonists had reorganized and kept shooting at the regulars.

From Concord the British, followed by the colonists, marched to Boston. This map shows the route they took. As they passed through Lexington on the way to Boston, the British set fire to the town. They fired cannons at the colonists, who fought back by firing their rifles at the British.

The Burning of Menotomy

The militia followed the regulars as they marched toward Boston Harbor. The militia formed a circle around the regulars and kept shooting at them. By the time they reached the town of Menotomy, the regulars were very angry. The colonists did not fight in the way the British were used to. Many of the regulars died, but the colonists were safely hidden. In Menotomy, the regulars burned houses, killing all of the people inside. Most of the women and children already had been moved to safety, but many people were killed. When the smoke cleared from the fighting in Menotomy, 25 colonists and at least 40 British soldiers were dead. What happened at Menotomy made many colonists think that the British were **savage** killers. As the stories about Menotomy spread, more and more colonists got ready for war with Great Britain.

Right: *Menotomy was on the road between Lexington and Boston.* Far right, top: *When the British arrived in Menotomy, they set the town on fire.* Far right, bottom: *This poster was made by a printer in Salem, Massachusetts, to show how many colonists were killed at Menotomy.* Right, inset: *A close-up of the poster shows rows of coffins, which represented the dead. This poster helped to convince the colonists to fight the British.*

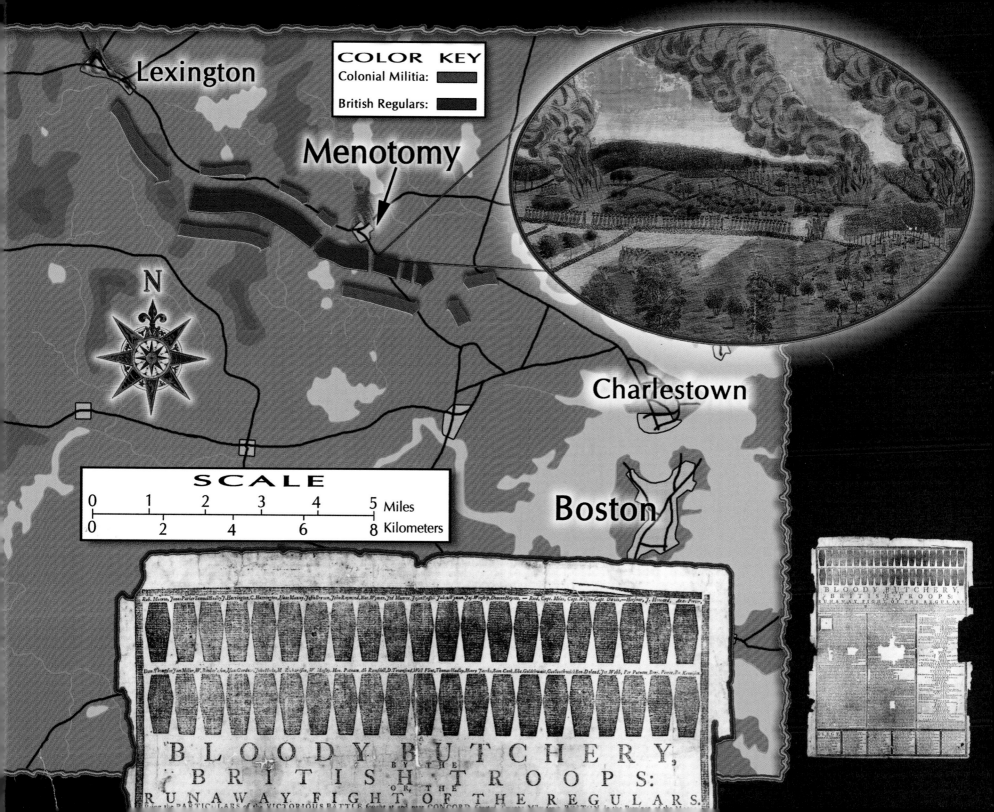

Lexington

Menotomy

Charlestown

Boston

COLOR KEY
Colonial Militia:
British Regulars:

N

SCALE

0	1	2	3	4	5	Miles
0		2		4	6	8	Kilometers

BLOODY BUTCHERY, BY THE BRITISH TROOPS: OR THE RUNAWAY FIGHT OF THE REGULARS.

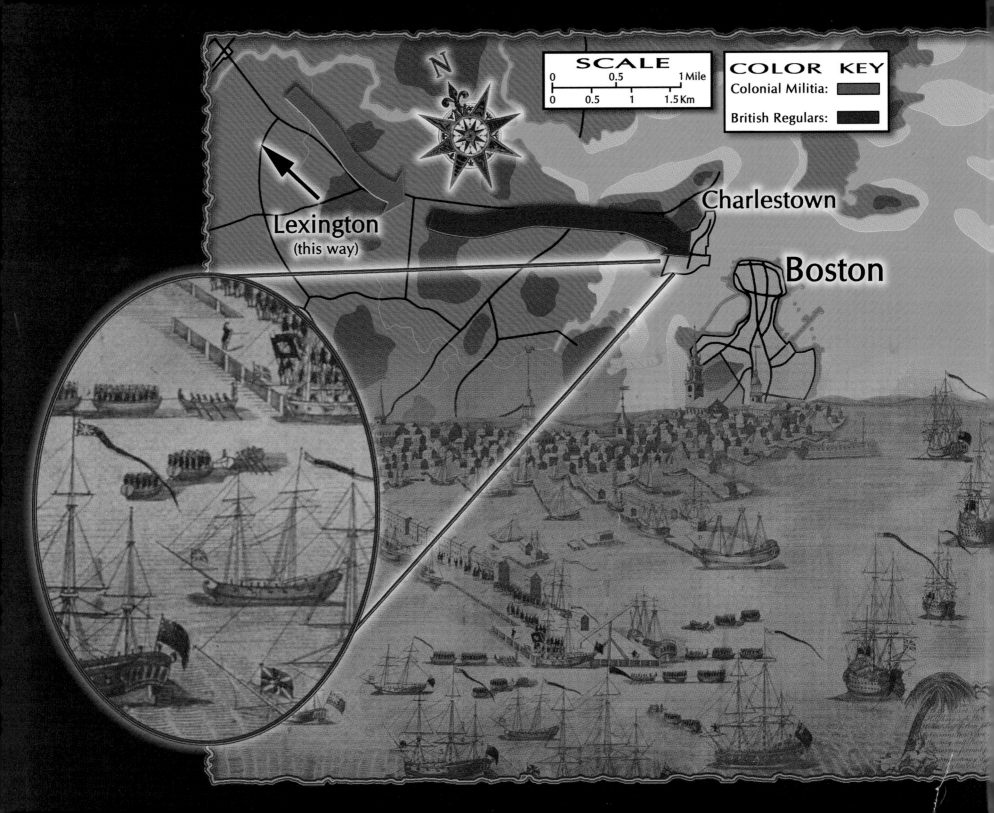

SCALE

0   0.5   1 Mile
0   0.5   1   1.5 Km

COLOR KEY

Colonial Militia:

British Regulars:

N

Lexington
(this way)

Charlestown

Boston

Counting the Dead

After sundown on April 19, 1775, the regulars reached the hills of Charlestown, near Boston. The colonists decided to stop their attack, because they did not want to be shot at by the cannons on the warships. In Charlestown the regulars got on small ships to go back to Boston Harbor, where larger ships were waiting for them. After a day of fighting, the regulars had 73 men dead, another 174 wounded, and 26 missing. On the colonists' side 49 people were dead, 40 were wounded, and 5 were missing. The colonists' losses were less than half of those suffered by the regulars. The battles at Lexington and Concord were finished, but the American Revolution had just begun. The day was a great victory for the colonists because they had proven that they could stand up to King George III.

This map shows the road the British took to Charlestown. Inset: Once they reached Charlestown, the British got on small boats, which took them to the warships that were anchored in Boston Harbor. At that time, the British had the most powerful navy in the world.

A Colony at War

Massachusetts was now officially at war with Great Britain. When news of the war reached the other colonies, more men arrived in Massachusetts to fight the regulars. Soon 16,000 colonists formed a half circle around Boston, trapping the regulars. At first some of the other colonies were doubtful about a war against Great Britain. Colonel Patrick Henry, the first governor of Virginia, made a famous speech in which he said, "Give me liberty or give me death!" This speech **convinced** many colonists to go to war. On May 10, 1775, leaders from every colony held a meeting to figure out what to do. They chose George Washington, a farmer from Virginia, to be the commander in chief of the Colonial army. The colonists still hoped only to gain equal rights from the king. It would take another year before they would want independence from Great Britain.

Glossary

colonists (KAH-luh-nists) People who live in a colony.

Continental Congress (kon-tin-EN-tul KON-gres) A group consisting of representatives from every colony who decided the actions of the colonies.

convinced (kun-VINSD) To have made a person believe something.

defied (dih-FYD) Stood up to authority.

disperse (dis-PURS) To move or to scatter something in all directions.

formation (for-MAY-shun) The way in which something is arranged.

governor (GUH-vuh-nur) An official who is put in charge of a colony by a king or queen.

massacre (MA-sih-ker) A fight in which many people on one side are killed.

militia (muh-LIH-shuh) A group of people who are trained and ready to fight in an emergency.

minutemen (MIH-net-men) Armed Americans who were ready to fight at a moment's notice.

musket (MUS-kit) A gun with a long barrel used in battle and hunting.

regulars (REH-gyuh-lurz) Professional British soldiers.

relief (ree-LEEF) A feeling of freedom from pain or difficulty.

retreat (ree-TREET) To back away from a fight.

savage (SA-vihj) Someone who is fierce, brutal, or cruel.

sniper (SNY-per) Someone who shoots at other people from a hidden position, usually a higher one.

submitted (sub-MIT-ed) Surrendered to the power, the control, or the authority of someone else.

techniques (tek-NEEKS) Special methods or systems used to do something.

weapons (WEH-puhns) Any objects or tools used to injure, disable, or kill.

Index

B

Boston Harbor, 5, 17–18, 21

Boston Massacre, 5

Boston Tea Party, 5

C

Continental Congress, 5

G

Gage, General Thomas, 6, 9

George III, king

of Great Britain, 5–6, 21

H

Henry, Colonel Patrick, 22

L

lanterns, 9

Lexington Green, 10

M

Menotomy, Massachusetts, 18

militia, 9, 13–14, 18

N

North Bridge, 13

P

Parker, Captain John, 10

Percy, General Lord Hugh, 17

Prescott, Samuel, 9

R

regulars, 5–6, 9–10, 13–14, 17–18, 21–22

Revere, Paul, 9

Primary Sources

Page 4. *Map of the 13 colonies.* This map was created by British map makers for King George III. It is now in the collection of the Map Division of the Library of Congress. **Page 7.** *General the Honourable Thomas Gage.* Oil on canvas, artist unknown, 1788. Yale Center for British Art, Paul Mellon Collection/USA/Bridgeman Art Library/New York. This is a detail of the original work, which was painted from life after Gage's return to Great Britain. **Page 8.** **(top)** *Samuel Prescott.* Print, artist and date unknown. Emmett Collection, Miriam and Ira D. Wallach Division of Arts, Prints and Photographs, The New York Pubic Library, Astor, Lenox and Tilden Foundations. Thomas Addis Emmett was an American doctor of the late nineteenth century. He donated his large collection of early American prints to the New York Public Library. **(bottom)** *Paul Revere.* Oil on canvas, John Singleton Copley, circa 1768–70. The Museum of Fine Arts, Boston. This is a detail of a work painted from life. As a symbol of his support of American independence Revere wears a shirt made from linen woven in the colonies. Weaving linen was illegal in the colonies. Instead the colonists were supposed to wear linen imported from Britain. **Page 11.** *The Battle of Lexington Green.* Engraving, Amos Doolittle, 1775. All Doolittle engravings, Print Collection, Miriam and Ira D. Wallach Division of Arts, Prints and Photographs, The New York Public Library, Astor, Lenox and Tilden Foundations. This is one a of a series of engravings made by the New Hampshire silversmith and engraver. The engravings are based on sketches Doolittle made two weeks after the Battle of Lexington and Concord. Doolittle made the sketches based on eye-witness accounts. **Page 12. (bottom)** *The Engagement at the North Bridge.* Detail of engraving, Amos Doolittle, 1775. **Page 19. (bottom)** *Bloody Butchery by the British Troops or the Runaway Flight of the Regulars.* Broadside. Ezekiel Russell, 1775. American Antiquarian Society. Russell was a Salem, Massachusetts printer. In the weeks following April 19, 1775, he printed at least six more editions of this broadsheet. It helped to turn public opinion against the British. **(top)** *A View of the South Part of Lexington.* Detail of engraving, Amos Doolittle, 1775.

Web Sites

Due to the changing nature of Internet links, PowerKids Press has developed an online list of Web sites related to the subject of this book. This site is updated regularly. Please use this link to access the list: www.powerkidslinks.com/afbar/lexcon/